Specials!

The Norman Conquest

Scott Reeves

Acknowledgements

© 2008 Folens Limited, on behalf of the author.

United Kingdom: Folens Publishers, Waterslade House, Thame Road, Haddenham, Buckinghamshire, HP17 8NT.
Email: folens@folens.com

Ireland: Folens Publishers, Greenhills Road, Tallaght, Dublin 24.
Email: info@folens.ie

Folens allows photocopying of pages marked 'copiable page' for educational use, providing that this use is within the confines of the purchasing institution. Copiable pages should not be declared in any return in respect of any photocopying licence.

Folens publications are protected by international copyright laws. All rights are reserved. The copyright of all materials in this publication, except where otherwise stated, remains the property of the publisher and the author. No part of this publication may be reproduced, stored in a retrieval system, or transmitted, in any form or by any means, for whatever purpose, without the written permission of Folens Limited.

Scott Reeves hereby asserts his moral right to be identified as the author of this work in accordance with the Copyright, Designs and Patents Act 1988.

Editor: Kayleigh Buller

Layout artist: Planman Technologies

Cover design: Martin Cross

Cover image: Mary Evans Picture Library

Illustrations: Katy Dynes

First published 2008 by Folens Limited.

Every effort has been made to contact copyright holders of material used in this publication. If any copyright holder has been overlooked, we should be pleased to make any necessary arrangements.

British Library Cataloguing in Publication Data. A catalogue record for this publication is available from the British Library.

ISBN 978-1-85008-364-1

Contents

Introduction	4
Edward the Confessor's England	5
England in the eleventh century (1)	6
England in the eleventh century (2)	7
England in the eleventh century (3)	8
Edward the Confessor	9
How would you describe Edward the Confessor?	10
Claiming the Throne	11
Harold Godwinson	12
Harald Hardrada	13
William of Normandy	14
1066 Blind Date (1)	15
1066 Blind Date (2)	16
Pick me!	17
Edgar the Atheling	18
1066 wordsearch	19
The Battle of Stamford Bridge	20
Harold vs Harald (1)	21
Harold vs Harald (2)	22
Saxon Chronicle	23
The Battle of Hastings	24
Harold vs William (1)	25
Harold vs William (2)	26
Why did William win? (1)	27
Why did William win? (2)	28
The death of King Harold	29
The Bayeux Tapestry	30
The Bayeux Tapestry	31
The story of 1066 (1)	32
The story of 1066 (2)	33
Fantastic facts	34
Finish the job!	35
The Harrying of the North	36
Rebels in the North (1)	37
Rebels in the North (2)	38
Orderic Vitalis	39
Rebels in the East	40
Hereward the Wake	41
The Feudal System	42
Sharing out the land (1)	43
Sharing out the land (2)	44
You are under arrest!	45
Role play cards (1)	46
Role play cards (2)	47
Castles	48
Motte and bailey castles (1)	49
Motte and bailey castles (2)	50
Stone castles	51
The Tower of London (1)	52
The Tower of London (2)	53
The Domesday Book	54
What was the Domesday Book?	55
True or false?	56
What did the Domesday Book tell the king?	57
William the Conqueror	58
How would you describe William? (1)	59
How would you describe William? (2)	60
How did others describe William?	61
The funeral of William the Conqueror	62
Norman Conquest wordsearch	63
Assessment sheet	64

Introduction

Specials! *History* have been specifically written for teachers to use with students who may struggle with some of the skills and concepts needed for Key Stage 3 History. The titles are part of a wider series from Folens for use with lower ability students.

Each book in the series contains ten separate units covering the topics needed to complete the theme of the book. Each unit has one or more photocopiable Resource sheets and several Activity sheets. This allows the teacher to work in different ways. The tasks are differentiated throughout the book and offer all students the opportunity to expand their skills. By using photocopiable writing frames and emphasising literacy skills, students will be able to access historical information more easily.

The teacher's notes give guidance and are laid out as follows:

Objectives
These are the main skills or knowledge to be learned.

Prior knowledge
This refers to the minimum skills or knowledge required by the students to complete the tasks. As a rule, students should have a reading comprehension age of 7 to 10 years and should be working at levels 2 to 4. Some activity pages are more challenging than others and you will need to select accordingly.

QCA and NC links
All units link to the QCA Schemes of Work and the NC for History at Key Stage 3 and the Northern Ireland PoS.

Background
This provides additional information for the teacher, expanding on historical details or giving further information about this unit.

Starter activity
Since the units can be taught as a lesson, a warm-up activity focusing on an aspect of the unit is suggested.

Resource sheets and Activity sheets
The Resource sheets, which are often visual but may also be written, do not include tasks and can be used as stimulus for discussion. Related tasks are provided on Activity sheets.

Where necessary, keywords are included on the student pages. Other keywords are included on the teacher's notes pages. These can be introduced to students at the teacher's discretion and depending on the students' ability.

Plenary
The teacher can use the suggestions here to recap on the main points covered or to reinforce a particular idea.

Look out for other titles in the History series, which include:
- *Specials! History* Native American Indians
- *Specials! History* The Tudors

Assessment sheet
At the end of the book, is an assessment sheet focusing on student progress. It can be used in different ways. A student can complete it as a self-assessment, while the teacher also completes one on each student's progress. They can then compare the two. This is useful in situations where the teacher or classroom assistant is working with one student. Alternatively, students can work in pairs to carry out peer assessments and then compare the outcomes with each other. Starting from a simple base that students can manage, the assessment sheet allows the student to discuss their own progress, to consider different points of view and to discuss how they might improve, thus enabling the teacher to see the work from the students perspective.

Teacher's notes

Edward the Confessor's England

Objectives

- To understand the geographical diversity in Europe at the end of the Saxon period
- Create historical judgements and interpretations

Prior knowledge

Students should be able to read text to seek basic information.

QCA link

Unit 2: How did medieval monarchs keep control?

NC links

2b: The social, cultural, religious and ethnic diversity of the societies studied, both in Britain and the wider world.
3a: How and why historical events, people, situations and changes have been interpreted in different ways.

Northern Ireland PoS

Study Unit 2: Rivalry and Conflict.

Resource sheets and Activity sheets

The Resource and Activity sheets titled, 'England in the eleventh century', require students to learn and consolidate their learning of the geographical and ethnic groups that will be central to the later chapters.

The Resource sheet titled, 'Edward the Confessor', provides information about the reign of Edward. Students should become familiar with his actions as king. This will enable them to make judgements about him using the Activity sheet, 'How would you describe Edward the Confessor?'.

Plenary

Recap the main keywords that students have used in this unit. Play a game (e.g. hangman) to consolidate understanding.

Background

Most students will begin this section of study with relatively little prior knowledge. They need to become aware of the Normans, Saxons and Vikings who will contest the throne in 1066 and the areas that they came from. Edward the Confessor (r.1042–1066) was a Saxon, but the four previous monarchs before him were Vikings. In addition, William of Normandy was descended from the seven previous Dukes, the first of whom was a Viking.

Starter activity

As a whole class, brainstorm 'The Norman Conquest'. Some students will know basic facts, e.g. The Battle of Hastings. Clarify any misunderstandings and explain that the class will begin to fill the gaps in their prior knowledge.

Resource sheet – Edward the Confessor's England

England in the eleventh century (1)

In the eleventh century England was quite a new country. England was formed when a group called the Saxons managed to unite the different English tribes into one country. The title 'King of England' had only existed for about 200 years, and it was invented by the Saxons.

However, not all of the kings of England had been Saxons. Some of the kings were Vikings from Norway and Denmark who had invaded and taken over England. The Vikings had been kings of England between 1013 and 1042.

There were also some Vikings who lived in northern France. This area was called Normandy, and these people were called Normans.

In 1042, a Saxon man called Edward the Confessor became the King of England. He was a popular king, who ruled the country well for 14 years.

The three groups in England were all interested in who would become the next king of England. The Saxons wanted one of their men to carry on being in charge. The Vikings said that they should have the throne back because they had it before Edward. The Normans were also interested because they thought that they might take charge. It was a tense time.

Resource sheet – Edward the Confessor's England

England in the eleventh century (2)

Activity sheet – Edward the Confessor's England

England in the eleventh century (3)

☞ Match each word up to the correct definition. One has already been done for you.

Heads	Tails
Edward the Confessor	A person who lived in northern France
King of England	An area where the Vikings lived
Norman	The title of the ruler of England
Norway	A group of people who lived in England
Saxon	A group of people who came from Denmark and Norway
Viking	The King of England between 1042 and 1066

(King of England is matched to "The title of the ruler of England")

Activity sheet – Edward the Confessor's England

Edward the Confessor

Edward the Confessor is remembered as a good king by most people. The Christian church decided that he was a saint, and he is the patron saint of the royal family.

Edward was born in 1003, and had to run away to Normandy when he was ten years old when the Vikings invaded England and took control of the country. As he grew up in Normandy, he became very religious, and made friends with many Normans.

In 1036, Edward invaded England and tried to win control of the country from the Vikings. However, his attack failed and he was forced to return to Normandy. His brother was captured by Earl Godwin and blinded by the King.

After the last Viking King of England died in 1042, Edward was invited to become the next King of England. His time as king was very peaceful. However, he had to keep people happy. His three most powerful subjects were Earls. They were called Earl Godwin, Earl Leofric and Earl Siward.

In 1051, Edward told Earl Godwin to leave England because he refused to punish somebody who had fought against Edward. Godwin returned a year later with an army and forced Edward to give him back his title and his land. Edward was lucky that Godwin died in 1053. He still worried that Godwin's son, Harold Godwinson, carried on building up the family's power.

Although Edward was married to Earl Godwin's daughter, he died in 1066 without any children. This meant there was no son to take over as the next King of England.

Activity sheet – Edward the Confessor's England

How would you describe Edward the Confessor?

☞ Below are different words that might be used to describe Edward the Confessor. Pick two that you agree with, and write in the boxes why you agree.

Strong	**Brave**

Clever	**Weak**

Teacher's notes

Claiming the Throne

Objectives

- Practice reading for information
- To communicate knowledge of the past through a speech
- To empathise with events and people in the past

Prior knowledge

Students should be able to read text to seek basic information.

QCA link

Unit 2: How did medieval monarchs keep control?

NC links

5c: Communicate their knowledge and understanding of history, using a range of techniques.

Northern Ireland PoS

Study Unit 2: Rivalry and Conflict.

Resource sheets and Activity sheets

The Resource sheets with the three contenders to the throne are intended for use with the Activity sheets titled, '1066 Blind Date (1)' and '(2)'. These allow students to familiarise themselves with the main personalities of the next few chapters. Students are required to record information that they find in the text. The Activity sheet, 'Pick me!', follows on from this, and requires students to present a persuasive argument.

The Activity sheet titled, 'Edgar the Atheling', considers a fourth claimant to the throne. Students should answer the two questions using the interview. This is also an opportunity for students to stretch themselves and give answers with a greater degree of explanation and thought. At the end of this unit students can complete the Activity sheet, '1066 wordsearch'.

Plenary

There is an opportunity for a class debate and vote. Of the three candidates (or four if Edgar the Atheling is included) who do they think should be the next King of England?

Background

There were no rules to decide the succession in 1066, the crown would go to the most powerful person who claimed the throne. It was unfortunate that Edward died with no heirs, and this led to the main claimants jockeying for position. The closest male heir, Edgar Atheling, was not considered a main contender because he was young, which meant that he lacked power. This was a good example of how power could overrule the line of succession.

Starter activity

Discuss how the UK is currently governed and who decides the government. The monarchy is a hereditary institution, and the government is decided in a democratic vote. Who would be in charge if there were no rules to decide it?

Resource sheet – Claiming the Throne

Harold Godwinson

When Edward the Confessor died, it was not clear who should be the next king. He did not have any children, and there were no rules to decide what should happen next.

The most powerful person in England was Harold Godwinson. He was the son of Earl Godwin, a very powerful person who had fought with Edward the Confessor when he was alive. Like Edward the Confessor, Harold was a Saxon, and he was the only contender who lived in England. He owned a lot of land, especially in Wessex where most of his supporters were.

Also, Harold was rich. He promised the people of England that he would not change anything and that they could keep all of their land and money.

Harold had a good claim to the throne. His sister was the wife of Edward the Confessor. Some people also think Edward told Harold to become king just before he died. However, Harold did not have royal blood himself, so would have to prove to everybody that he was the best man to be the next king.

Resource sheet – Claiming the Throne

Harald Hardrada

Apart from Harold Godwinson, another man called Harald wanted to become king too, but his name was spelled slightly differently. Harald Hardrada was the King of Norway, and was a great warrior. Many people in the North of England were descended from Vikings, and these people would have wanted a Norwegian Viking to be the King of England.

Harald was already rich because he was the king of another country. He did not need to make money, so there was no fear that he would take the land from most English people.

Harald wanted to become king because Vikings had been the Kings of England between 1013 and 1042, and he thought that Edward had stolen the throne from them. However, the Vikings had invaded England when they became kings, so the Saxons said that it was the Vikings who had stolen the throne, not them. Some people were nervous that the Vikings would invade again.

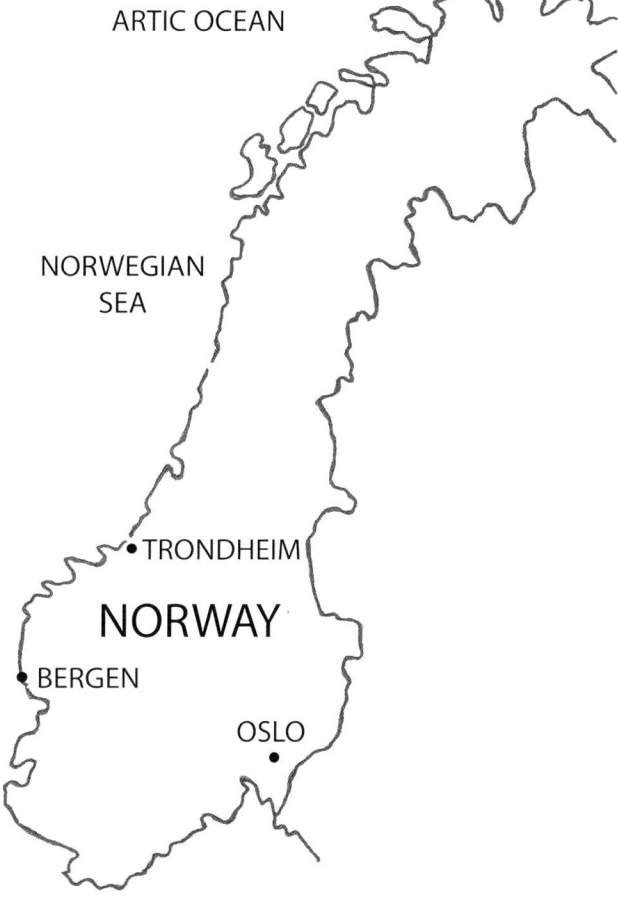

Resource sheet – Claiming the Throne

William of Normandy

The final person who wanted to be king after Edward died was William. He was the Duke of Normandy in northern France.

William was friends with Edward the Confessor, because Edward had grown up in Normandy when the Vikings were ruling England. William claimed that Edward was so thankful to the Normans that he had promised William the throne of England when he died.

William had written to the Pope (the leader of the Church) to tell him about the problem of who would be the next English king. The Pope had promised William the support of the Church.

However, William was not very rich – and this meant that he would take land and use the English to collect taxes to make him richer. The English people would not be happy if William won and made them poor!

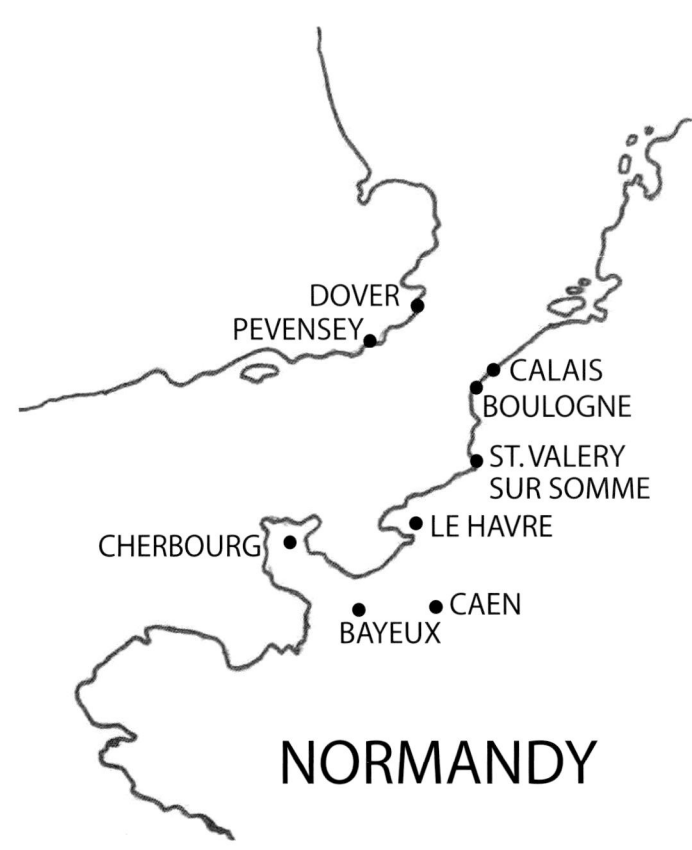

Activity sheet – Claiming the Throne
1066 Blind Date (1)

☞ Imagine that the English people are allowed to choose who will be their next king. They might decide to get all of the potential candidates to answer three questions similar to the television programme Blind Date. Using the information on the Resource sheet, answer the questions for each candidate.

	Harold Godwinson
Why should you be king?	
Who are your friends and allies?	
What will you do with England?	

Activity sheet – Claiming the Throne
1066 Blind Date (2)

William, Duke of Normandy	
Why should you be king?	
Who are your friends and allies?	
What will you do with England?	

Harald Hardrada, King of Norway	
Why should you be king?	
Who are your friends and allies?	
What will you do with England?	

Activity sheet – Claiming the Throne

Pick me!

Pick one of the three contenders for the throne: Harold Godwinson, Harald Hardrada or William of Normandy.

☞ You need to write a speech that will persuade the people of England to vote for your chosen person. Write your speech in the scroll provided.

Remember, you are trying to persuade people that your contender is the best. You should include all of the good things about your person, but do not mention the bad things. You can also say what is bad about the other contenders, but do not say what their good points are.

Activity sheet – Claiming the Throne

Edgar the Atheling

The closest relative to Edward the Confessor in 1066 was Edgar the Atheling, he was not really considered to be the next king. What would he have said?

> I was born in Hungary, and my great-uncle was Edward the Confessor, the King of England. I was his closest male relation when he died, so really I should have been the next king. However, I was only 15 years old, and people did not think that a child was strong enough to lead the country. I'd have liked the chance to prove them wrong!
>
> After 1066, I tried to fight the King of England. I raised an army with the help of the Kings of Scotland and Denmark and invaded. They were both weak, but they were the best people who supported me. Although I lost, the King forgave me. I also fought against the English Kings in 1087 and 1106, but I always seemed to pick the wrong side to support. Each time, the kings were good enough to forgive me again.
>
> I also travelled around Scotland, and went to fight for the Church in the First Crusade. When I die, I expect people will remember me as the King of England who never sat on the throne!

☞ 1 Why do you think Edgar never became King of England?

☞ 2 Why do you think Edgar was well treated by the kings of England after 1066?

Write your answers on a separate piece of paper.

Activity sheet – Claiming the Throne

1066 wordsearch

☞ In this wordsearch you will find the names of all of the people who claimed the throne, as well as the king who had just died. Can you find them all?

You will also find the names of two important places. Can you find them?

All the words appear either down or across.

G	V	H	M	G	M	G	N	B	M	C	N	A	F	W
F	O	S	C	R	L	A	F	E	D	W	A	R	D	Q
N	L	V	O	R	T	A	P	F	I	J	I	S	X	P
H	S	F	E	I	A	I	W	T	E	E	U	O	Q	V
A	E	V	O	R	S	N	I	S	C	D	U	L	O	Z
R	J	N	L	Y	N	T	L	Z	N	Z	V	U	G	O
A	A	O	I	U	I	M	L	M	A	H	A	T	P	L
L	I	R	O	T	F	P	I	V	R	N	E	E	U	D
D	L	W	S	F	I	H	A	R	O	L	D	F	U	P
E	F	A	C	S	R	M	M	X	T	W	G	S	B	S
P	O	Y	Y	L	B	M	E	S	S	A	A	I	V	V
C	T	R	E	N	O	L	U	T	I	O	R	C	R	B
D	E	Z	T	L	O	U	I	S	L	E	F	O	P	D
P	Y	D	R	N	O	R	M	A	N	D	Y	E	I	H
Y	L	S	D	V	S	I	H	L	R	D	U	K	V	X

WILLIAM   EDWARD

HAROLD   NORWAY

HARALD   NORMANDY

EDGAR

Teacher's notes

The Battle of Stamford Bridge

Objectives
- To practice putting events in chronological order
- To communicate knowledge of the past in a newspaper report

Prior knowledge
Students should be able to read text to seek basic information.

QCA link
Unit 2: How did medieval monarchs keep control?

NC links
5b: Accurately select and use chronological conventions and historical vocabulary appropriate to the periods studied to organise historical information.
5c: Communicate their knowledge and understanding of history, using a range of techniques.

Northern Ireland PoS
Study Unit 2: Rivalry and Conflict.

Background

The Battle of Stamford Bridge on 25 September 1066 was a decisive victory for Harold Godwinson. This happened because King Harold's army marched to the north in four days, and King Harold was able to surprise Harald Hardrada. However, this battle also meant that Harold lost valuable soldiers and time that would contribute to his defeat at Hastings.

Starter activity

Discuss the one-sidedness of sources. A good example is to imagine a football match report from a team's own programme or magazine after they have won 1-0 with a controversial penalty. It is likely to be one-sided and support the team – praising the team rather than describing the win as lucky.

Resource sheets and Activity sheets

The Resource and Activity sheets titled, 'Harold vs Harald', are designed to be used together. Students are given basic information about the battle and must put five statements into chronological order. This can be extended by asking students to design a storyboard or cartoon strip for the battle using these statements as headings.

The Activity sheet called, 'Saxon Chronicle', requires students to describe what happened at the battle, but also to use purposely one-sided language to give a biased account. This activity will enable students to gain a good understanding of what happened.

Plenary

Discuss the usefulness of written sources relating the football example from the starter activity to the Saxon Chronicle newspaper report. Make clear to students that written sources are not always reliable because they might have a one-sided point of view.

Resource sheet – The Battle of Stamford Bridge

Harold vs Harald (1)

Soon after the death of Edward the Confessor, Harold Godwinson, who was in the best position to act, had himself crowned King of England. If anybody else wanted to become king, they would have to fight him for it.

Harald Hardrada decided to invade England with his army from Norway. He brought 10 000 warriors on 300 ships. Hardrada landed somewhere in the North East, and marched his army to York. He also had help from Tostig, Harold Godwinson's younger brother.

Hearing this, Harold Godwinson (now King Harold) marched an army up to meet them. King Harold's army moved quickly, and surprised Hardrada at Stamford Bridge near York. Some of Hardrada's army did not have their armour with them because they were not expecting to fight.

At the battle, some of the Vikings fought bravely. One warrior managed to kill lots of King Harold's men on a bridge. To get him, men from Harold's army floated underneath the bridge and stabbed him from below. King Harold and his army also managed to kill Harald Hardrada and Tostig, who was chopped into pieces.

It is said that King Harold's army fought so well that only four ships were needed to take the Vikings back to Norway.

Activity sheet – The Battle of Stamford Bridge

Harold vs Harald (2)

☞ Put these statements in the correct order: 1 being the beginning of the story, 5 being the end. One has already been done for you.

| Hardrada landed somewhere in the North East, and marched his army to York | |

| Only four ships were needed to take the Vikings back to Norway | |

| King Harold and his army managed to kill Harald Hardrada and Tostig | |

| Harold Godwinson had himself crowned King of England | 1 |

| King Harold's army moved quickly, and surprised Hardrada at Stamford Bridge | |

Activity sheet – The Battle of Stamford Bridge

Saxon Chronicle

Newspapers were not invented in 1066. For this task, you need to imagine that they were.

You are a reporter who writes for a newspaper called the Saxon Chronicle. The editor of your newspaper thinks that King Harold is the best man to be the King of England. He thinks that the result of the Battle of Stamford Bridge was excellent.

☞ You need to tell your readers what happened at the battle. You also need to use language that shows that you like the result of the battle. Try using as many words from the word box as you can. Make sure you have a catchy headline and an interesting picture to go with your article.

The Saxon Chronicle

| brave | excellent | glory | tremendous | triumph |

© Folens (copiable page)   The Norman Conquest

Teacher's notes

The Battle of Hastings

Objectives
- To categorise the causes of an event
- To evaluate the reliability of sources

Prior knowledge
Students should be able to read text to seek basic information.

QCA link
Unit 2: How did medieval monarchs keep control?

NC links
2c: Analyse and explain the reasons for, and results of, the historical events, situations and changes in the periods studied.
4b: Evaluate the sources used, select and record information relevant to the enquiry and reach conclusions.

Northern Ireland PoS
Study Unit 2: Rivalry and Conflict.

Background

The Battle of Hastings, on 14 October 1066, was the pivotal moment of the Norman Conquest. As medieval battles go, it was a huge incident, lasting for most of the day and seeing charge after charge by the Normans. Victory was William's, but the result could have been different had decisions (and luck) turned out differently. After the battle, with Harold and Harald dead, William's position as King of England was secure.

Starter activity

Discuss causation as a class. Use an analogy to draw out understanding that events can have more than one cause: for example a footballer might move abroad because he wants to win a European championship *and* because he wants to live in a sunnier country.

Resource sheets and Activity sheets

The Resource sheets titled, 'Harold vs William', give a simplified version of the events of the battle. The Resource and Activity sheets titled, 'Why did William win?', require students to categorise the causes of William's victory.

The Activity sheet, 'The death of King Harold', is designed to help students practice evaluating the reliability of sources. Students need to highlight two sources and question their reliability. The Norman monk, although writing relatively soon after the battle, may have been one sided as he came from Normandy. The modern novel is likely to exaggerate or change things to make the story more exciting and dramatic, and may have been influenced by the Bayeux Tapestry, the reliability of which is discussed in a different chapter.

Plenary

Discuss the reasons behind William's victory, referring back to the discussion in the starter activity. Explain that William's victory had two causes: his leadership and Harold's mistakes.

Resource sheet – The Battle of Hastings

Harold vs William (1)

William, Duke of Normandy, invaded England with his army of Norman soldiers in September 1066. William's army was very well prepared. The Norman army included archers with longbows and cavalry (soldiers on horseback).

When King Harold heard about the invasion, he immediately marched his soldiers down to the south coast from Yorkshire, where they had been fighting Harald Hardrada. Harold's long march south took about two weeks, and he lost many men who were tired and slow.

King Harold had also let some of his men go home because it was harvest time. They needed to collect their crops. If Harold did not let them go, he thought that they would run away and never come back.

The two sides met each other at Hastings. King Harold managed to line his army up at the top of Senlac Hill. William had a worse position, his men were at the bottom of the hill. It looked like Harold would win the battle.

© Folens (copiable page)   The Norman Conquest

Resource sheet – The Battle of Hastings

Harold vs William (2)

After hours of fighting, King Harold was still safe on the top of the hill. William had not worked out a way to win the battle. The Norman army kept charging against King Harold's army, but they kept on being beaten back down the hill.

During the fighting, William led his army from the front. At one point, William lifted up his helmet to show his troops that he was in the middle of the fighting to encourage them.

Eventually, William had a plan. His army pretended to run away. Some of King Harold's army ran down the hill to chase them, but William's men turned around and killed them. William's army pretended to run away three times. Each time, more of Harold's army was killed.

Towards the end of the day, King Harold's two brothers were killed. King Harold was killed, possibly by an arrow in his eye or by Norman cavalry. The rest of his army fled, and William had won!

Resource sheet – The Battle of Hastings
Why did William win? (1)

William's army was very well prepared.

William's army pretended to run away three times. Each time, more of Harold's army was killed.

The Norman army included archers with longbows and cavalry (soldiers on horseback).

William lifted up his helmet to show his troops that he was in the middle of the fighting to encourage them.

Harold's long march south took about two weeks, and he lost many men who were tired and slow.

King Harold had let some of his men go home because it was harvest time.

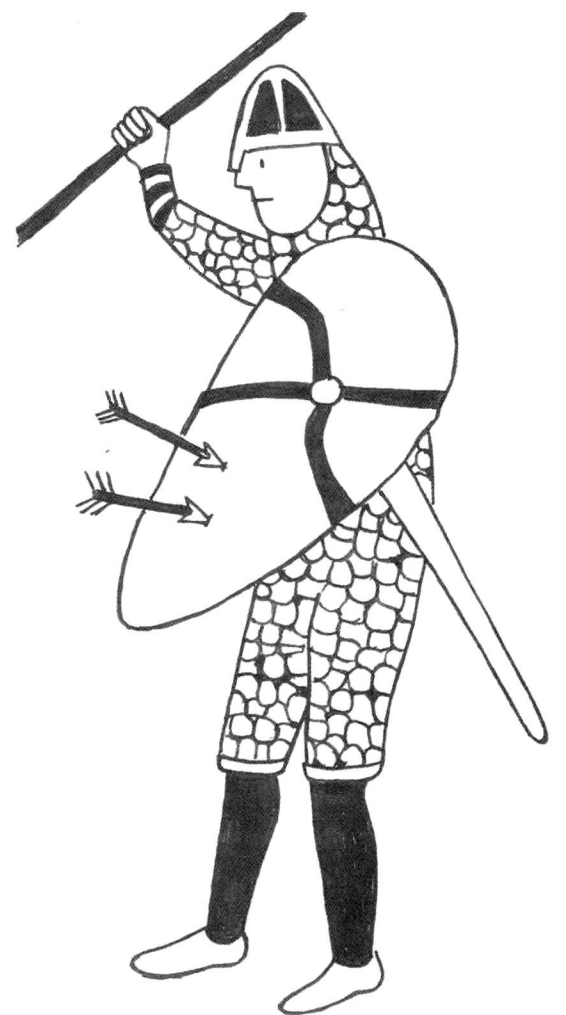

Activity sheet – The Battle of Hastings

Why did William win? (2)

☞ 1 Look at the causes of William's victory in the Battle of Hastings. You need to decide which ones are about William's leadership and which ones are about Harold's mistakes. Put them into the correct box.

William's leadership – things that the Normans did well	Harold's mistakes – things that he did wrong

☞ 2 Which of these two categories do you think was the most important? Why? Write your answer on a separate piece of paper.

Activity sheet – The Battle of Hastings

The death of King Harold

People disagree about what happened to King Harold at the Battle of Hastings. Pictures drawn after the event are unclear, and might not have been made by people who were there.

☞ Read the two descriptions about Harolds death. Do you think either is likely to contain the truth?

> With the point of his lance the first knight pierced Harold's shield and chest, drenching the ground with blood. With his sword the second knight cut off his head. The third disembowelled him with his javelin. The fourth hacked off his leg.
> (A Norman monk writing in 1068)

> One of the arrows struck Harold, putting out one of his eyes. He then dropped his battleaxe to the ground as he wrenched the arrow from the sightless eye and broke it in two with his powerful hands. Then he bent over his shield. Twenty mounted knights charged straight at the royal party. One struck with his spear, penetrating the King's shield and breast. A second sent Harold to the ground with a slash of his sword. The King, dying, struggled to rise. The third knight ripped out his guts with a spear, while the sword of a fourth cut open his thigh.
> (From a historical novel published in 1973)

☞ Answer the following questions on a separate piece of paper.

1 Highlight, in each source, the words that describe how Harold was killed.
2 What do the sources agree about?
3 What do the sources disagree about?
4 Which of these sources is most likely to contain the truth? Explain your answer.

Teacher's notes

The Bayeux Tapestry

Objectives

- To evaluate the reliability of sources

Prior knowledge

Students should have some knowledge of Harold Godwinson, William of Normandy and the Battle of Hastings.

QCA link

Unit 2: How did medieval monarchs keep control?

NC links

4b: Evaluate the sources used, select and record information relevant to the enquiry and reach conclusions.

Northern Ireland PoS

Study Unit 2: Rivalry and Conflict.

Background

The Bayeux Tapestry is a large pictorial source showing the events of 1066. It was probably created in the 1070s and was commissioned by Odo, the Bishop of Bayeux, and the half-brother of William. Although the source offers valuable and detailed information on the Norman Conquest, its reliability as a source must be considered. Was Odo boasting about his family's success, and his own by association? Are some of the details unclear or have they lost their meaning over time?

Starter activity

The Activity sheet titled, 'The Bayeux Tapestry', is useful as a starter activity. It is designed to have students study closely pictorial sources. It will familiarise students with the type of pictorial source they will encounter in this section.

Resource sheets and Activity sheets

The Activity sheets titled, 'The story of 1066 (1)' and '(2)', require students to analyse the sections of the tapestry in more detail. An alternative is to approach this as a cut-and-stick task, this will add greater challenge as students will have eight possible answers for each picture rather than four.

The Activity sheet, 'Fantastic facts', requires the highest level thinking in this section. Students need to consider the reliability of the Bayeux Tapestry as a source by considering who paid for, designed and made it. These questions can form the basis of a discussion or written work.

The Activity sheet, 'Finish the job!', gives students a chance to complete the missing section of the Bayeux Tapestry, enabling them to consider in more depth the planning and detail that was needed to go into the original design and construction.

Plenary

Play 'Keyword Countdown', students have 30 seconds to unscramble the following keywords from this section: YEA BUX (Bayeux), SIGN TASH (Hastings) and STRUT (trust).

Activity sheet – The Bayeux Tapestry

The Bayeux Tapestry

Sometime after the Battle of Hastings, probably in the 1070s, the Bayeux Tapestry was made. It is a little bit like a cartoon strip, and shows the events of 1066 including the Battle of Hastings.

☞ Label this section of the Bayeux Tapestry. One has already been done for you.

Arrow in Harold's eye

Long shield to protect legs

Rex (Latin for King)

Soldier being stripped of his armour

Knight on horseback

Battle axe

© Folens (copiable page)   The Norman Conquest   31

Activity sheet – The Bayeux Tapestry

The story of 1066 (1)

☞ Draw a line connecting each section of the Bayeux Tapestry with the correct label. One has already been done for you.

The Normans sail across the English Channel

Harold swears loyalty to William

William and his men have a feast

Harold is crowned King of England

Activity sheet – The Bayeux Tapestry
The story of 1066 (2)

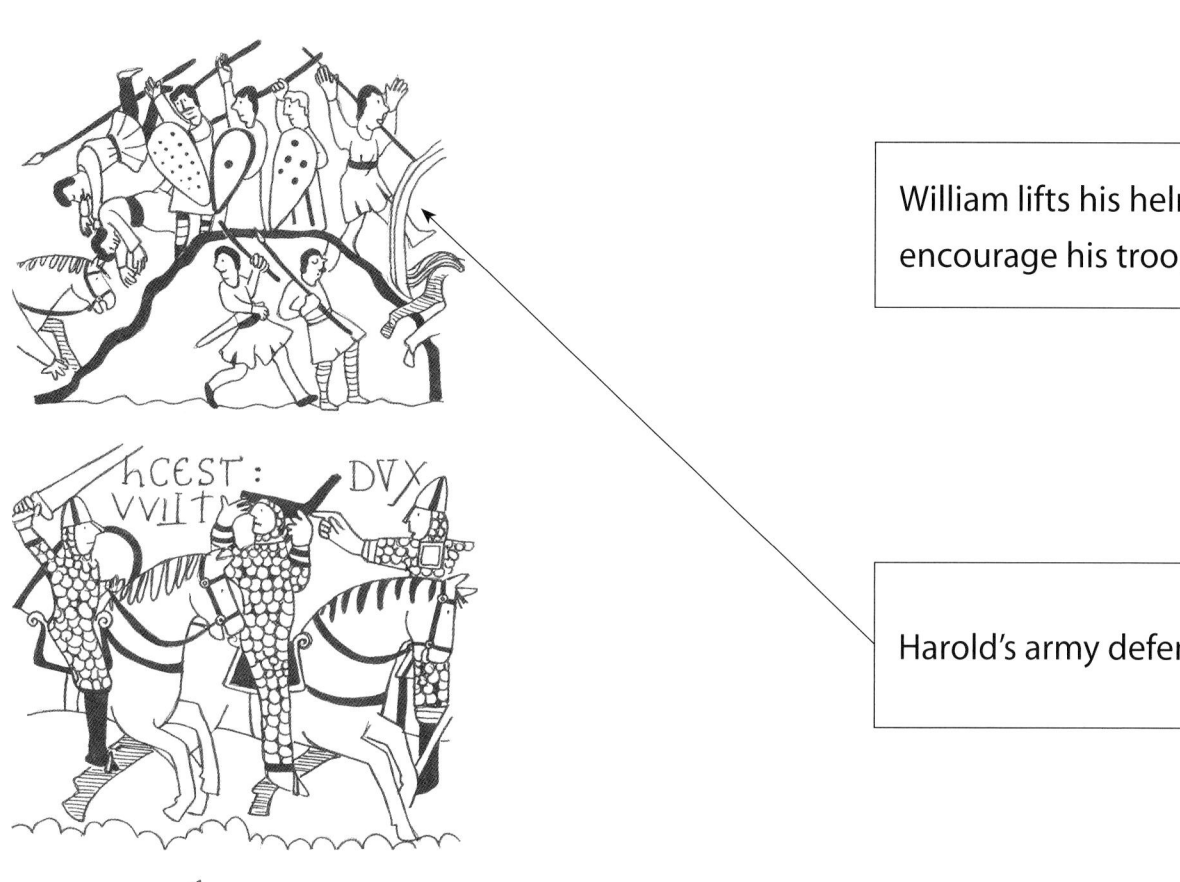

William lifts his helmet to encourage his troops

Harold's army defends a hill

The Norman cavalry chases Harold's army away

Harold is killed

© Folens (copiable page)   The Norman Conquest

Activity sheet – The Bayeux Tapestry

Fantastic facts

| The Bayeux Tapestry is not a tapestry (something woven, like a carpet), but an embroidery (something sewn, like the initials on a handkerchief). |

| It includes 623 people, 202 horses, 41 ships and 55 dogs. |

| People have questioned who designed the tapestry. Many of the scenes are very personal, like the death scene of Edward the Confessor, and would have only been seen by someone very close to royalty. |

| There is a panel with a religious person hitting a woman. Nobody knows the meaning of this scene. |

| Many historians have argued over who made the tapestry. Some people claim it was made by French people in Bayeux. Some think that the tapestry was made by English people in Kent. |

| There are more than 500 mythical creatures along the borders. |

| The tapestry is over 70 metres long, so it is about the length of three swimming pools. |

| The tapestry was probably paid for by Odo of Bayeux, the half-brother of William the Conqueror. Odo was a bishop and travelled with William during the Norman invasion. |

| There are some very detailed and accurate combat scenes, so presumably the designer had first hand knowledge of the Battle of Hastings itself. |

☞ 1 Are there any reasons why historians *can* trust the Bayeux Tapestry? Highlight the facts that help you explain your answer.

☞ 2 Are there any reasons why historians *cannot* trust the Bayeux Tapestry? Highlight the facts that help you explain your answer in a different colour.

Activity sheet – The Bayeux Tapestry

Finish the job!

Not a lot of people know that part of the Bayeux Tapestry is actually missing. About eight metres have disappeared and have never been seen by historians. We don't know what was shown but some have guessed there were pictures of William's coronation and the Normans building castles.

☞ You need to design the missing section of the tapestry using this template.

Teacher's notes

The Harrying of the North

Objectives
- To evaluate the reliability of sources

Prior knowledge
Students should be able to read text to seek basic information and be aware of William's success at Hastings.

QCA link
Unit 2: How did medieval monarchs keep control?

NC links
4b: Evaluate the sources used, select and record information relevant to the enquiry and reach conclusions.

Northern Ireland PoS
Study Unit 2: Rivalry and Conflict.

Background

Although William was almost certain to be crowned after his victory at Hastings, he was not secure in his position. Numerous rebellions arose during his first years as king. This section concentrates on the rebellion of Edwin and Morcar that led to the Harrying of the North and the rebellion of Hereward the Wake in East Anglia. Each time, William was ruthless and used force to ensure that he stayed in power.

Starter activity

Define the words 'fact' and 'opinion'. Give examples from everyday life, students must decide whether they are facts or opinions, for example: 'physics is a science' and 'history is a great subject'.

Resource sheets and Activity sheets

The Resource sheets, 'Rebels in the North' and 'Rebels in the East', give information that will enable students to complete the tasks on the Activity sheets in this section.

The Activity sheet titled, 'Oderic Vitalis', enables students to question and evaluate the point of view of a written source. This source was written by a monk, and students should evaluate the source and question whether it was somebody who was unsympathetic to William, perhaps somebody who lost friends or family in the Harrying of the North.

The Activity sheet titled, 'Hereward the Wake', requires students to identify three facts and three opinions about Hereward, and to explain which opinion they find the most convincing.

Plenary

Write down one fact ("Edwin and Morcar rebelled against William") and one opinion ("Hereward the Wake was a hero") that students can remember from the lesson.

Resource sheet – The Harrying of the North

Rebels in the North (1)

When William won the Battle of Hastings in 1066, he knew that he was not secure as the King of England. Even when he was crowned on Christmas Day in 1066, people were fighting in the streets outside. William knew that he would have to fight people who did not accept him.

In 1069, the people that William had asked to look after the north of England decided to rebel and fight against him. They were called Edwin and Morcar, and they had help from an army that came from Denmark. They killed hundreds of William's supporters in York.

William sent an army to the north of England, but the rebels ran away. To punish the people in the north, William attacked lots of villages. He burned houses and crops and killed animals. This attack was known as the Harrying of the North.

Even if they were not killed by the soldiers, people in the north were not safe. William had taken away their food, so thousands of people died of starvation. The north of England took decades to recover from the attack.

Resource sheet – The Harrying of the North

Rebels in the North (2)

In 1087, nearly 20 years after the Harrying of the North, people went around England writing down what the country was like. Lots of places were described as 'waste' because there was nothing there after William's soldiers had destroyed them. Look at the map below and see how many places William destroyed in the Harrying of the North.

Activity sheet – The Harrying of the North

Orderic Vitalis

One person who wrote down what happened during the Norman Conquest was a monk called Orderic Vitalis. One of his parents was English and one of them was Norman. He had very strong feelings about the Harrying of the North. You can tell this in this section of his writing.

> The King stopped at nothing to hunt his enemies. He cut down many people and destroyed many homes and land. Nowhere else had he shown such cruelty. To his shame he made no effort to control his fury and he punished the innocent with the guilty. He ordered that crops and animals, tools and food should be burned to ashes. More than 100 000 people perished of hunger. I can say nothing good about this brutal slaughter. God will punish him.
> (Orderic Vitalis, written about 1125)

☞ 1 Highlight any words that make the Harrying of the North sound like a bad event.

☞ 2 Do you think that the person who wrote this down thought that William was a good king?

☞ 3 Can you think of any reasons why you might not be able to trust this person?

Explain your answers on a separate piece of paper.

Resource sheet – The Harrying of the North

Rebels in the East

The most famous Englishman who fought against William was called Hereward the Wake. He came from a family who owned land before the Norman Conquest, but William took their land from them and killed his brother. When he found out about this, Hereward is said to have killed 15 Norman soldiers and put their heads on spikes outside his old house.

Hereward then travelled to Ely in East Anglia. The land around there was wet and marshy, and William found it difficult to attack with his army. They needed to use rafts to get across the watery land, and Hereward used traps to kill them.

William eventually got his army into Ely, and took control of the area. They killed many of Hereward's supporters and took a lot of money away.

Hereward killed his favourite horse because he did not want the Normans to take her. Nobody knows exactly what happened to Hereward. Some people think that William was so impressed with his bravery that he let Hereward go, but it is more likely that he ran away.

Activity sheet – The Harrying of the North

Hereward the Wake

A fact is an event or something that happened.
An opinion is what a person thinks about something.

| Hereward killed 15 men when he heard that his brother was dead. |

| Hereward travelled to Ely in East Anglia. |

| Hereward was a hero. |

| Hereward killed his horse because he did not want her to be captured. |

| Hereward was a coward because he hid from the Norman army. |

| Hereward was brave because he stood up to William even though he was the king. |

☞ 1 Colour any boxes that are facts in green.
☞ 2 Colour any boxes that are opinions in red.
☞ 3 Which of the opinions do you agree with the most? Explain your answer on a separate piece of paper.

Teacher's notes

The Feudal System

Objectives

- Communicate knowledge of the past through a written description and a representational model

Prior knowledge

Students should be able to read text to seek basic information.

QCA link

Unit 2: How did medieval monarchs keep control?

NC links

5c: Communicate their knowledge and understanding of history, using a range of techniques.

Northern Ireland PoS

Study Unit 2: Rivalry and Conflict.

Background

The feudal system allowed William to keep control of the country. It was a structured hierarchy that allowed power to dissolve down the system. This meant that no individual became too powerful, and William could call on an army at times when he was threatened. Although not mentioned in this section, the feudal system also contained the church – bishops and abbots were landowners roughly equivalent to the level of the barons and knights.

Starter activity

Describe a hierarchy of authority that students are familiar with. For example, explain that a school is under the control of a head teacher, but responsibility is delegated to teachers, and students have the least influence and power.

Resource sheets and Activity sheets

The Resource sheet titled, 'Sharing out the land', gives a simplified explanation of the feudal system. The Activity sheet of the same title allows students to consolidate knowledge and understanding of the feudal system. The Activity sheet, 'You are under arrest!', requires students to communicate knowledge in the form of a written description.

The Resource sheets titled, 'Role play cards (1)' and '(2)', can be cut out and stuck onto an A3 sheet to show the system.

Plenary

The Activity sheets titled, 'Role play cards (1)' and '(2)', give an opportunity to create a physical representation of the feudal system. Students can be given a card and should organise themselves to show the feudal system. The king could be stood on a table, the barons sat on the table, the knights sat on a chair and the peasants sat on a floor.

Resource sheet – The Feudal System

Sharing out the land (1)

Although he was the King of England, William could not personally visit everywhere to make sure that people were loyal to him and were doing what he wanted. Rebellions against him in the north of England and in East Anglia were proof that he needed to have people who supported him around the country. To make this happen, William put in place the feudal system.

As the King of England, William owned all of the land. He gave out large areas of land to his most loyal followers called the barons. In return, the barons promised to help him rule the country. There were about 200 barons.

The barons had to share out the land that they had been given. They gave smaller sections of land called manors to the knights. The knights promised to fight for the king when the barons asked them to. There were about 1000 knights.

The knights had to share out the land that they had been given. They gave small plots of land to the peasants. The peasants had to farm the land and grow food. There were a lot of peasants – about 100 0000 of them.

If anybody in the system chose to rebel against William, he had plenty of other people who were willing to fight for him – and he could then take the land from the rebels and give it to somebody else.

Activity sheet – The Feudal System

Sharing out the land (2)

☞ Complete the diagram by putting the most powerful group at the top and the least powerful group at the bottom.

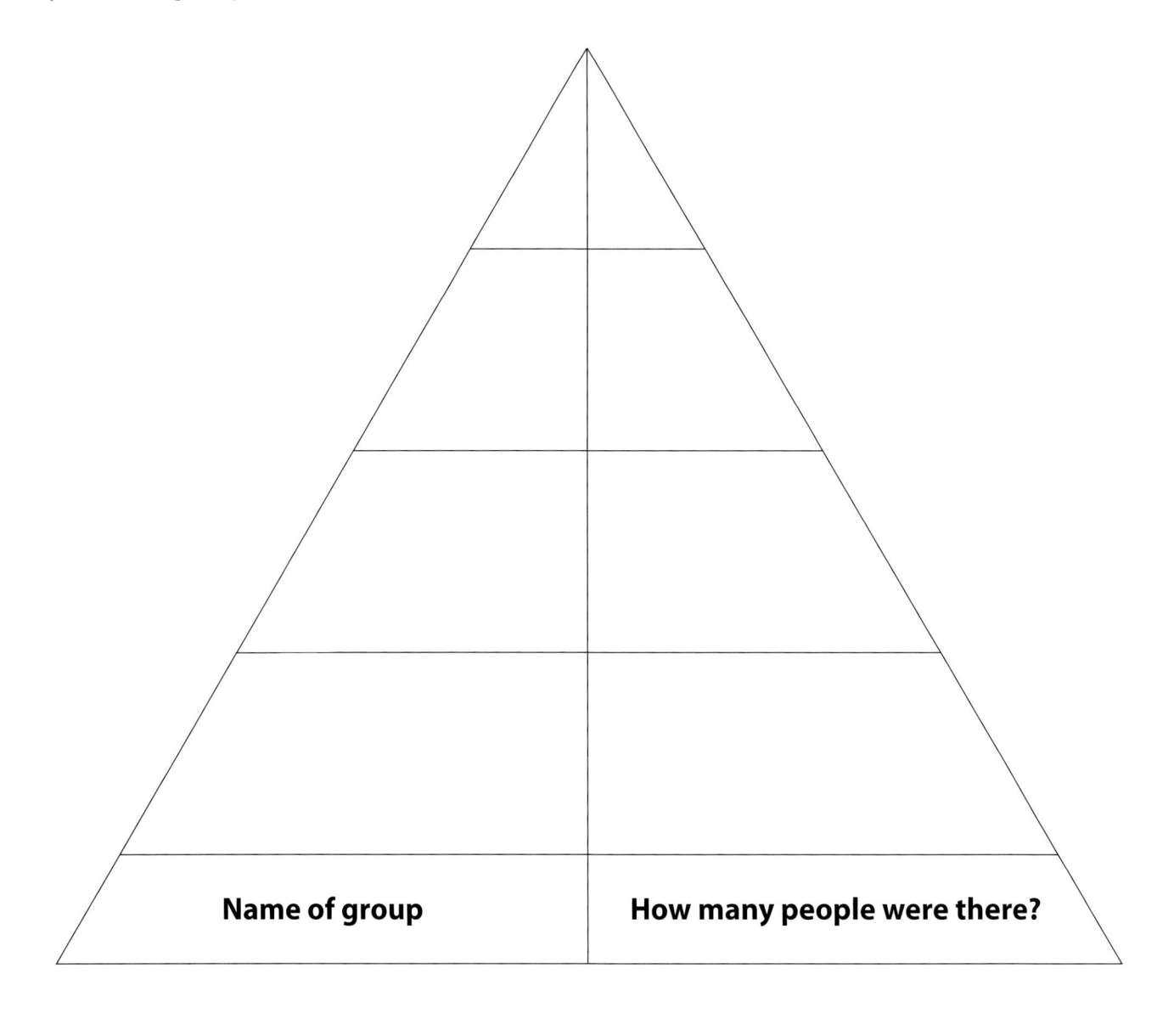

Name of group	**How many people were there?**

| King | Knights | Barons | Peasants |

| 1000 | 1 | 100 000 | 200 |

The Norman Conquest

Activity sheet – The Feudal System

You are under arrest!

It is 1070, and you are a knight living happily in England. Suddenly, there is a bang on the door, it is some of William's soldiers, and they have heard that you are planning a rebellion!

☞ The soldiers say that they will let you go if you can prove your loyalty. They want you to describe the feudal system to them. They are short on time, so you must do it in **less than 100 words** (that is about the length of these instructions). They also insist you mention the words at the bottom of the page.

Quickly, before you are taken to the Tower of London!

| feudal | king | baron | knight | peasant |

© Folens (copiable page) — The Norman Conquest

Resource sheet – The Feudal System
Role play cards (1)

King William
You run the country!

Knight Neil
Your job is to fight for the king and the barons

Baron Bertie
Your job is to help the king run the country

Knight Neville
Your job is to fight for the king and the barons

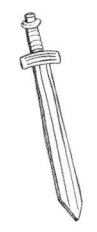

Baron Billy
Your job is to help the king run the country

Knight Nigel
Your job is to fight for the king and the barons

Baron Boris
Your job is to help the king run the country

Knight Norman
Your job is to fight for the king and the barons

Resource sheet – The Feudal System

Role play cards (2)

Peasant Paddy
Your job is to grow food for the knights

Peasant Perry
Your job is to grow food for the knights

Peasant Paul
Your job is to grow food for the knights

Peasant Peter
Your job is to grow food for the knights

Peasant Percy
Your job is to grow food for the knights

Peasant Pradeep
Your job is to grow food for the knights

Peasant Peregrin
Your job is to grow food for the knights

Peasant Preston
Your job is to grow food for the knights

Teacher's notes

Castles

Objectives
- To understand similarities and differences

Prior knowledge
Students should be able to read text for basic information and be aware of the barons and the feudal system.

QCA link
Unit 2: How did medieval monarchs keep control?

NC links
2d: Identify trends.

Northern Ireland PoS
Study Unit 2: Rivalry and Conflict.

Background

Castles were King William's attempt to stay in control of a particular area. Fortifications had been built in England since prehistory, but the Normans were the first to build castles as we know them. However, under the Normans, castle building changed a great deal. Early motte and bailey castles were built out of wood, and were superseded by stone castles. Also, stone castles changed in their design and construction throughout the medieval period.

Starter activity

As a whole class, brainstorm 'Castles'. It is likely that students will have a particular view of castles (thinking only of stone castles). Explain that this section of work will look at how castles changed.

Resource sheets and Activity sheets

The Resource sheet titled, 'Motte and bailey castles (1)' and '(2)', gives students information about the first castles built by the Normans. The Activity sheet of the same title allows students to consolidate this knowledge.

The Resource and Activity sheets titled, 'The Tower of London', are designed to be used together. These give students an opportunity to identify change and continuity.

Plenary

Play 'Keyword Jeopardy' – the teacher gives three answers, and students must think of a suitable question that matches: MOTTE, BAILEY, KEEP.

Resource sheet – Castles

Motte and bailey castles (1)

When William and his army had taken over an area, he needed to make sure he kept control. The best way of doing this was to build a castle.

The castles that you can see now are big and built of stone. They took years to build. When he was taking control of the country, William needed castles quickly. The first type of castle that he built was called a motte and bailey castle.

The motte was the big mound that made the castle difficult to attack, and also meant that the people in the castle could see farther. The section where the baron lived was built on top of the motte, and it was called a keep. Around the outside of the castle was a fence called a palisade. Inside the fence was a courtyard called a bailey.

Motte and bailey castles helped William take control of the country. They were cheap and quick to build. However, they did not last forever. They would eventually rot, or if they were attacked they could be burned down. If William wanted to stay in control, he would have to build castles out of stone.

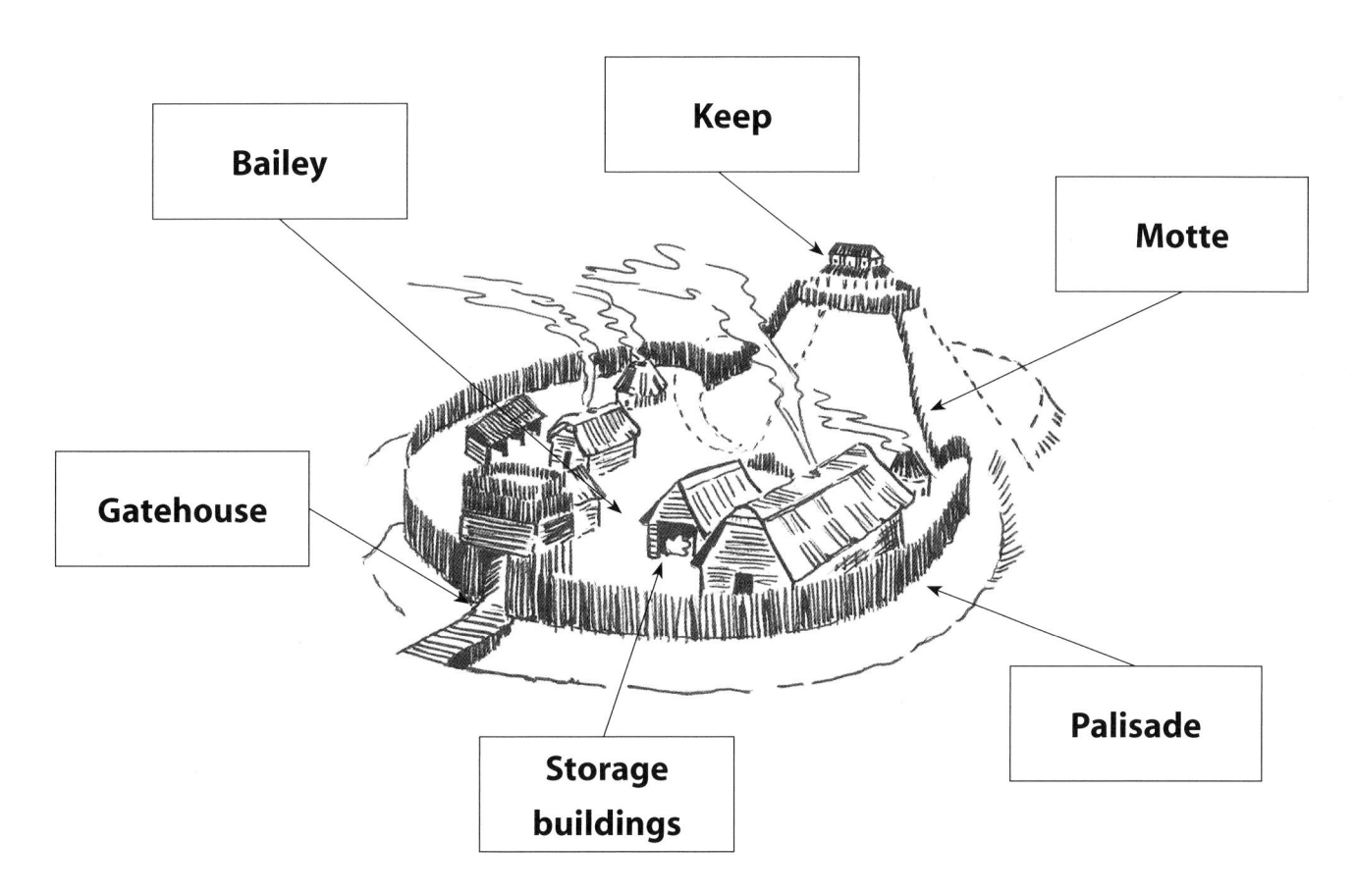

Activity sheet – Castles

Motte and bailey castles (2)

☞ Match each part of the castle up to the correct definition. One has already been done for you.

Heads	Tails
Bailey	Large fence around the castle
Gatehouse	Main section of castle where the baron would live
Keep	Strong point at the entrance to the castle
Motte	Where the castle supplies were kept in case the castle was attacked
Palisade	Courtyard inside the fence
Storage buildings	Large mound of earth

(Gatehouse is matched to "Strong point at the entrance to the castle".)

Resource sheet – Castles

Stone castles

Once William felt like he was in control of an area, he began to replace his wooden motte and bailey castles with ones built out of stone. Each stone castle was different depending on what the baron who lived in it wanted, and how much money he had.

All stone castles had a keep where the baron lived. Around the castle was usually a strong stone wall with gaps on top that the soldiers could fire arrows through. These gaps were called battlements. Along the wall would be round towers. They were harder to knock down than square towers because they had no corners.

The entrance to the castle was usually guarded with a barbican. It might also have a strong metal gate called a portcullis. The barbican was sometimes booby-trapped, so attackers might fall into a pit underneath. Sometimes they had a murder hole above them and the castle defenders could pour boiling water or tar onto any attackers.

Stone castles were not perfect, and attackers could sometimes get in. However, it might take several weeks, and this would give time for the king to come to the rescue with a bigger army!

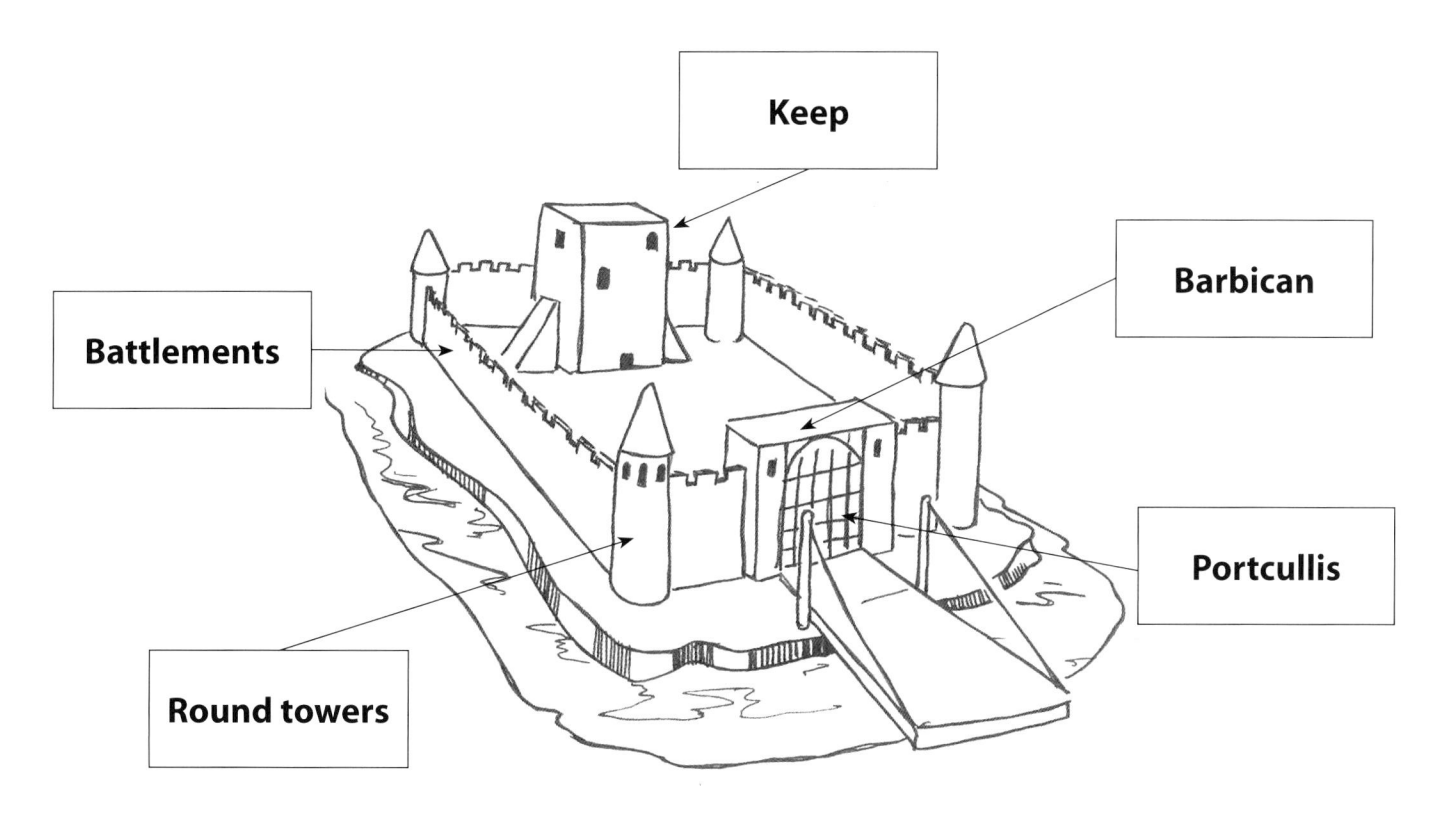

Resource sheet – Castles

The Tower of London (1)

One of the most famous castles in Britain is the Tower of London. It was built in the reign of King William, and was changed by the kings who followed. It changed so much that after 200 years King William would not have recognised it. Can you spot the changes in the pictures?

The Tower of London in 1100

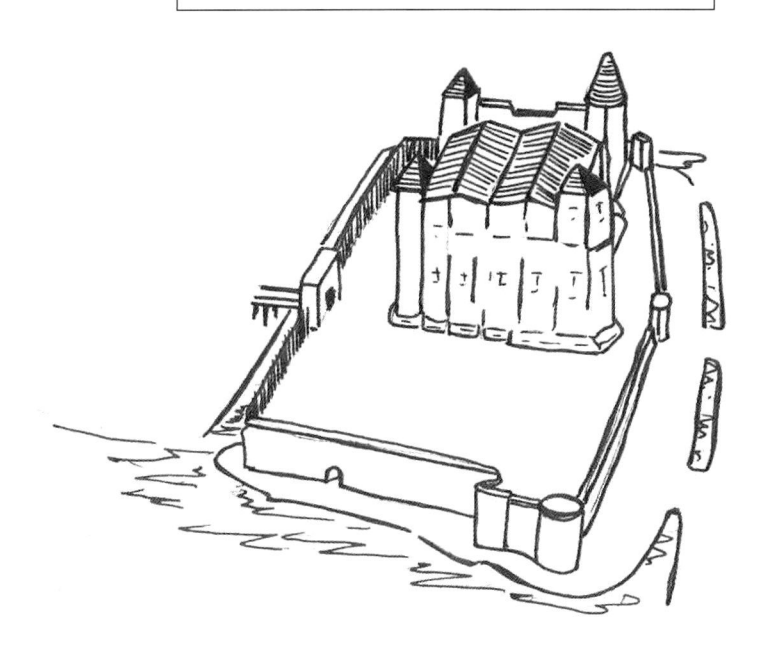

The Tower of London in 1300

Activity sheet – Castles

The Tower of London (2)

☞ Use the table below to record differences and similarities between the two different pictures of the Tower of London.

Stayed the same	Changed

There are two walls for extra protection.

There is a stone keep in the middle where the baron would live.

There are lots of towers.

There is a moat filled with water around the castle.

There is a large courtyard with extra buildings in.

There are extra courtyards.

© Folens (copiable page)   The Norman Conquest

Teacher's notes

The Domesday Book

Objectives
- To evaluate the reliability of sources

Prior knowledge
Students should be able to read text to seek basic information.

QCA link
Unit 2: How did medieval monarchs keep control?

NC links
4b: Evaluate the sources used, select and record information relevant to the enquiry and reach conclusions.

Northern Ireland PoS
Study Unit 2: Rivalry and Conflict.

Background

The Domesday Book was William's large scale survey of his new kingdom, designed to allow him to tax the country at a suitable rate. It is an excellent source for historians of the period, although it focuses on land and money and only reveals glimpses of social history.

Starter activity

Begin the lesson speaking only in French, students will find it difficult or impossible to understand you! Explain that this is a situation that the conquering Normans will have found in England, and the English may have resented their conquerors.

Resource sheets and Activity sheets

The Activity sheet, 'True or false?', aims to consolidate knowledge and understanding of the Domesday Book that students gained from the Resource sheet titled, 'What was the Domesday Book?'. Students could be encouraged to work together as a team to find the answers, or to compete against each other in a 'penalty shoot-out' format. The true answers are Q.2, 4, 5, 7.

The Activity sheet titled, 'What did the Domesday Book tell the king?', allows students to analyse an extract from the Domesday Book for a village in Sussex. Students should be able to identify basic information, and then begin to question the information in it. Patcham seems to have suffered under the Norman Conquest and was presumably damaged by fighting or rebellion.

Plenary

Refer back to the starter activity, now that students are aware of the Domesday survey, they can appreciate the difficulties that the inspectors must have found when they were surveying an unfamiliar country. Remember, even if the inspectors spoke English, the range of accents in medieval England was very broad.

Resource sheet – The Domesday Book

What was the Domesday Book?

By the end of his reign, William felt secure as King of England. He had defeated the people who fought against him, built castles to control areas and had his men in charge of the land. Now he wanted to know what he could do with his country.

In 1086, William sent out men with orders for them to collect information about every place in the country. They interviewed people in every village and town, and wrote down what they were told. They wanted to know how big the places were, who was in charge and how much the land was worth. The name 'Domesday' means judgement, so the Domesday Book is the 'Book of Judgement'.

The inspectors visited 13 418 different places. They wrote down that there were 48 castles and 60 monasteries.

They found out that the King controlled 17% of the land. Twenty six percent was owned by the church, and 54% of the land was owned by 190 barons. Only two of the barons had owned land before the Norman Conquest. They were called Thorkhill of Arden and Coleswain of Lincoln.

Some women were mentioned too. The most important one was Countess Judith, the niece of William. Queen Edith (Edward the Confessor's wife) and Queen Matilda (William's wife) were also mentioned, but they were both dead.

William wanted to use the book so he knew how much money there was in England and who he could tax. However, he did not live to use it, he died in 1087, and the book was not completed until after this.

© Folens (copiable page)   The Norman Conquest

Activity sheet – The Domesday Book

True or false?

☞ Read the following statements below. Decide whether they are true or false. Tick the correct box to show your answers.

		True	False
1	William wanted a book because he did not have anything to read.	☐	☐
2	The Domesday survey began in 1086.	☐	☐
3	The 'Domesday Book' means 'Book of Death'.	☐	☐
4	The inspectors visited 13 418 different places.	☐	☐
5	The King owned 17% of the land.	☐	☐
6	The Church did not own any land in England.	☐	☐
7	There were about 190 barons who owned land.	☐	☐
8	Coleswain of Liverpool was one of two landowners before 1066 who was still alive in 1086.	☐	☐
9	Only one woman was mentioned in the Domesday Book.	☐	☐
10	The Domesday Book won an award because it was such a good story.	☐	☐

Activity sheet – The Domesday Book

What did the Domesday Book tell the king?

This is a typical extract from the Domesday Book. It describes the village of Patcham in Sussex.

> 'In the area around Preston, King William holds Patcham himself. Earl Harold held it before 1066. Then there was room for 60 families; now for 40. There is land for 80 ploughs. The King has eight ploughs; the 163 villagers and 45 smallholders have 82 ploughs. There is a church; six slaves; ten shepherds; a meadow of 84 acres; woodland with 100 pigs; and 26 sites worth 13 shillings. Richard has enough land for seven families; and a knight of his has land for half a family. In lordship they have two ploughs, with two smallholders. Total value before 1066: £100; later: £50; now: £80.'

1 Read the extract above and answer these questions on a separate piece of paper.

1 Who owned Patcham before 1066?
2 Who owned Patcham after 1066?
3 How many ploughs are there in Patcham?
4 What do you think the woodland was used for?
5 Why do you think the value of the land dropped after 1066?
6 Imagine you want to find out about the life of a peasant. Do you think that the Domesday Book would be a good source to use?

Teacher's notes

William the Conqueror

Objectives
- To create historical judgements and interpretations
- To evaluate the reliability of sources
- Practice reading for information

Prior knowledge
Students should have a general understanding of the reign of William the Conqueror.

QCA link
Unit 2: How did medieval monarchs keep control?

NC links
3a: How and why historical events, people, situations and changes have been interpreted in different ways.
4b: Evaluate the sources used, select and record information relevant to the enquiry and reach conclusions.

Northern Ireland PoS
Study Unit 2: Rivalry and Conflict.

Background
William the Conqueror is a central part of early medieval history. This section focuses on William's impact, students must consider whether his legacy was good or bad, and also consider the views of contemporaries.

Starter activity
Introduce the idea of historical judgements and interpretations. If students had to give themselves a nickname that said something about them (e.g. a William the Conqueror style nickname might become Victoria the Talkative in a school setting), what would it be?

Resource sheets and Activity sheets
Students should be familiar with the events of the Norman Conquest. This will enable them to make judgements about William the Conqueror using the Activity sheets, 'How would you describe William?'. Students should also use their knowledge to assess the judgements of two contemporaries of Henry on the Activity sheet, 'How did others describe William?'.

The Activity sheet titled, 'The funeral of William the Conqueror' completes William's story with a description of his funeral. Students should highlight the text to practice seeking information from text.

Plenary
As a whole class, brainstorm 'Norman Conquest'. Students should be able to provide a fairly comprehensive outline of the period. Students should be given an opportunity to compare their brainstorm to an earlier activity at the start of their work in Chapter 1 (Edward the Confessor's England) if they completed it.

Activity sheet – William the Conqueror

How would you describe William? (1)

There is no doubt that William had a massive effect on England. He won the Battle of Hastings and gained control through the Harrying of the North. He also built castles, introduced the feudal system and organised the Domesday Book. He was given the nickname 'Conqueror', because he conquered (took over) England.

☞ Below are different words that might be used to describe William the Conqueror. Pick four that you agree with, and write in the boxes why you agree.

Strong

Brave

Clever

Cruel

Activity sheet – William the Conqueror

How would you describe William? (2)

Weak	Good Leader

Determined	Important

Activity sheet – William the Conqueror

How did others describe William?

Not everybody has the same opinion about events and people in the past. A good historian needs to be able to look at opinions and work out which ones they think are the most reliable or truthful.

Some people liked William, and some people did not. Which of these two opinions do you think is the most reliable?

> King William loved gold and silver and did not care how sinfully it was obtained provided it came to him. He did not care at all how wrongfully his men got possession of land or how many illegal acts they did.
> (From the Anglo-Saxon Chronicle, a diary written by an unknown monk in England around 1087)

> William never allowed himself to be turned from any task because of the work it involved. He was strong in body and tall in stature. He was moderate in drinking, for he hated drunkenness in all men. In speech he was fluent and persuasive, being skilled at all times in making clear what he wanted. He followed the Christian religion in which he had been brought up from childhood, and whenever his health permitted he regularly attended Christian worship each morning and at the celebration of mass.
> (From a book by William of Jumieges, a monk who lived in Normandy)

☞ 1 Highlight any positive words in each statement in one colour. Then highlight any negative words in a different colour. Is each source mainly positive or negative about William?

☞ 2 Which of these sources do you think is the most reliable (most likely to tell the truth)? Explain your answer on a separate piece of paper.

Activity sheet – William the Conqueror

The funeral of William the Conqueror

☞ 1 How did William die? Highlight it in this source:

William was on his way to Rouen, and on the way attacked a French army at Mantes. The battle was hard, and many buildings were ruined. William passed one on horseback, but his horse shied away from the burning fire, and threw him violently in the saddle. His stomach hit the front of the saddle. He hit it so hard that his intestines burst and waste matter began to poison him. He slowly died over five weeks.

☞ 2 Highlight the phrase in this source that suggests that William's funeral was not usual:

William died at daybreak on September 9, in his 60th year, and was buried in rather unseemly fashion in St Stephen's Church, which he had built at Caen.

☞ 3 So what happened? Highlight the unusual thing that happened:

His body was carried to his great church of St Stephen at Caen. Towards the end of his life he had grown very fat, and when the attendants tried to force the body into the stone sarcophagus, it burst, filling the church with a foul smell. It was an unfortunate ending to the career of an unusually fortunate and competent king.

☞ 4 What was the reaction of the people? Highlight it in this source:

A group of bishops applied pressure on the king's abdomen to force the body downward into the coffin, but it moved only inches; the lid still would not shut. Again they pushed, and the abdominal wall, already under intense internal pressure, burst. Pus and putrefaction drenched the king's death garb and seeped throughout the coffin. The stench so overpowered chapel mourners that, hands to noses, many raced for the doors.

Activity sheet – William the Conqueror

Norman Conquest wordsearch

☞ You have learned a lot of keywords in this section of work. Can you find them in this wordsearch? The words will appear either down or across.

You need to find:

BAYEUX	FEUDAL	MOTTE
CASTLE	HARALD	NORMANDY
CONQUEROR	HAROLD	REBELLION
DOMESDAY	HASTINGS	WILLIAM
EDWARD	KEEP	

G	V	H	A	R	A	L	D	B	M	C	N	A	F	W
F	O	S	C	A	S	T	L	E	D	O	N	B	K	I
N	L	V	O	N	T	A	P	F	E	N	F	A	L	L
L	S	F	M	I	A	I	E	T	L	A	N	Y	P	L
J	E	D	O	M	E	S	D	A	Y	N	L	E	N	I
R	H	N	T	Y	N	T	W	R	Z	A	P	U	P	A
Z	A	A	T	U	I	M	A	M	A	R	Y	X	F	M
L	S	Z	E	T	F	P	R	Y	B	D	H	E	U	D
F	T	T	S	F	I	I	D	I	E	L	A	F	U	P
E	I	N	C	O	N	Q	U	E	R	O	R	Y	B	S
U	N	P	Y	L	A	P	N	W	H	Y	O	F	V	V
D	G	R	E	B	E	L	L	I	O	N	L	G	R	B
A	S	Z	T	L	O	U	I	S	L	E	D	F	P	D
L	Y	L	R	N	O	R	M	A	N	D	Y	E	I	H
Y	L	S	D	V	S	I	H	L	R	D	K	E	E	P

Assessment sheet – The Norman Conquest

✓ Tick the boxes to show what you know.

I know:

	Yes	Not sure	Don't know
what England was like in 1066			
who wanted to be King of England after Edward			
what happened at Stamford Bridge			
why William won the Battle of Hastings			
whether the Bayeux Tapestry is useful			
how William dealt with rebellions			
what the Feudal system was			
how castles changed			
how reliable the Domesday Book was			
whether William the Conqueror was a good king			

The thing that I remember most is:

_____

_____

I need to work on (up to three targets):

1 _____

2 _____

3 _____